YOUR AMAZING BODY

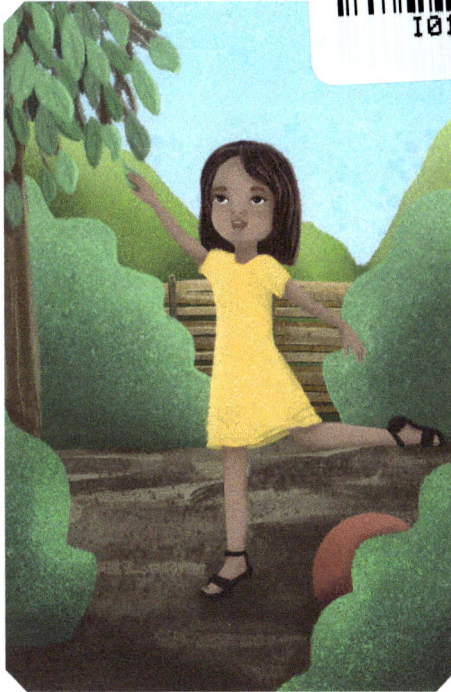

By JOwen

Library For All Ltd.

LIBRARY FOR ALL

DIGITAL EDUCATION FOR THE WORLD

Library For All is an Australian not for profit organisation with a mission to make knowledge accessible to all via an innovative digital library solution. Visit us at libraryforall.org

Your Amazing Body

First published 2022

Published by Library For All Ltd
Email: info@libraryforall.org
URL: libraryforall.org

Our Yarning logo design by Jason Lee, Bidjipidji Art

Original illustrations by Mila Aydingoz

Your Amazing Body
JOwen
ISBN: 978-1-922827-52-4
SKU01402

YOUR AMAZING BODY

We respect and honour Aboriginal and Torres Strait Islander Elders past, present and future. We acknowledge the stories, traditions and living cultures of Aboriginal and Torres Strait Islander peoples on this land and commit to building a brighter future together.

Your body is amazing.

Do you know how it works?

HEAD

HAIR

NECK

SHOULDERS

4

Let's start at the top.
Can you point to your
head
hair
neck and
shoulders?

EYES

EARS

NOSE

TEETH

MOUTH

Now let's talk about your
face. Can you point to your
eyes
ears
nose
teeth and
mouth?

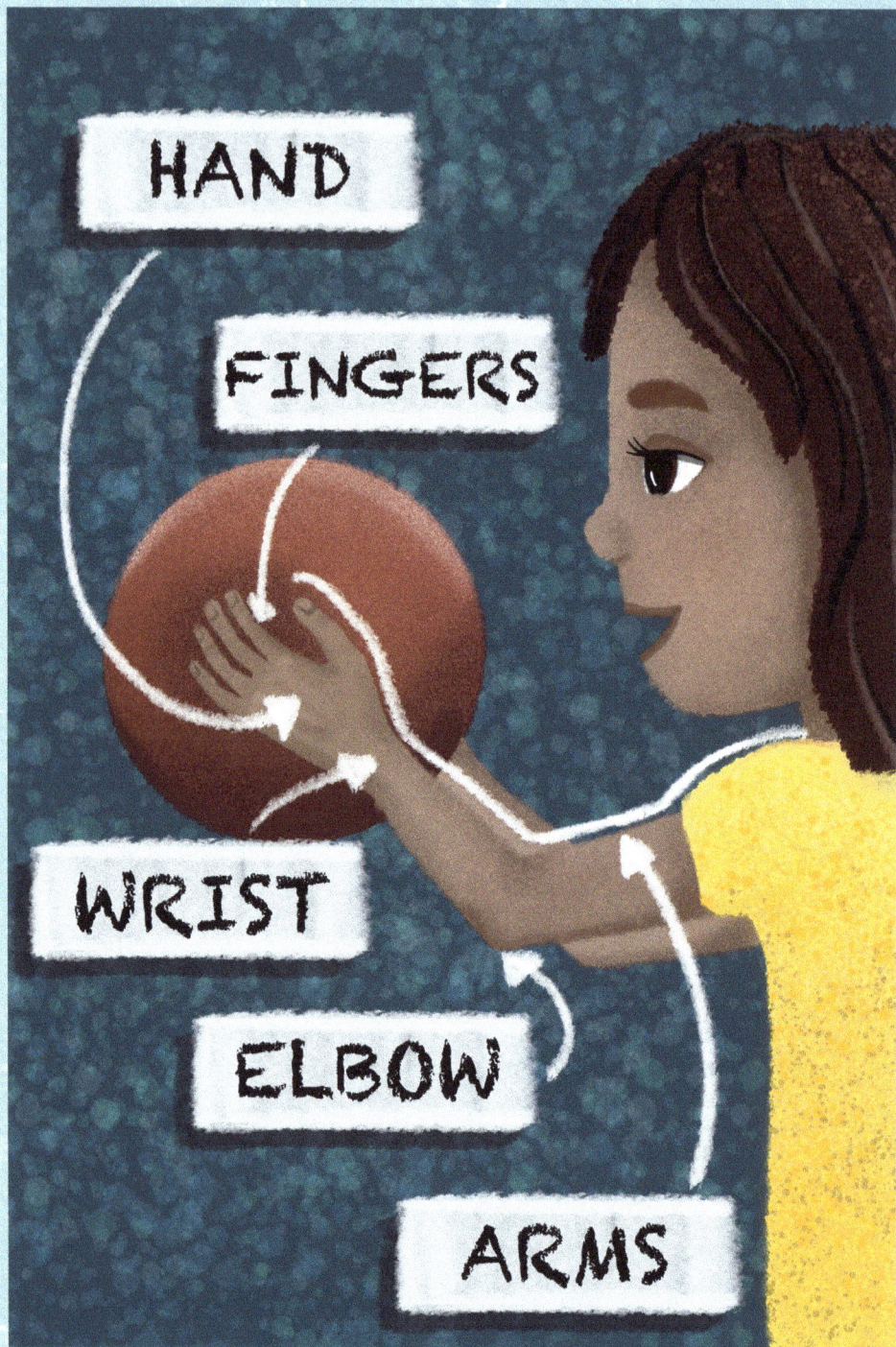

HAND

FINGERS

WRIST

ELBOW

ARMS

8

Next, can you point to your
arms
elbows
wrists
hands and
fingers?

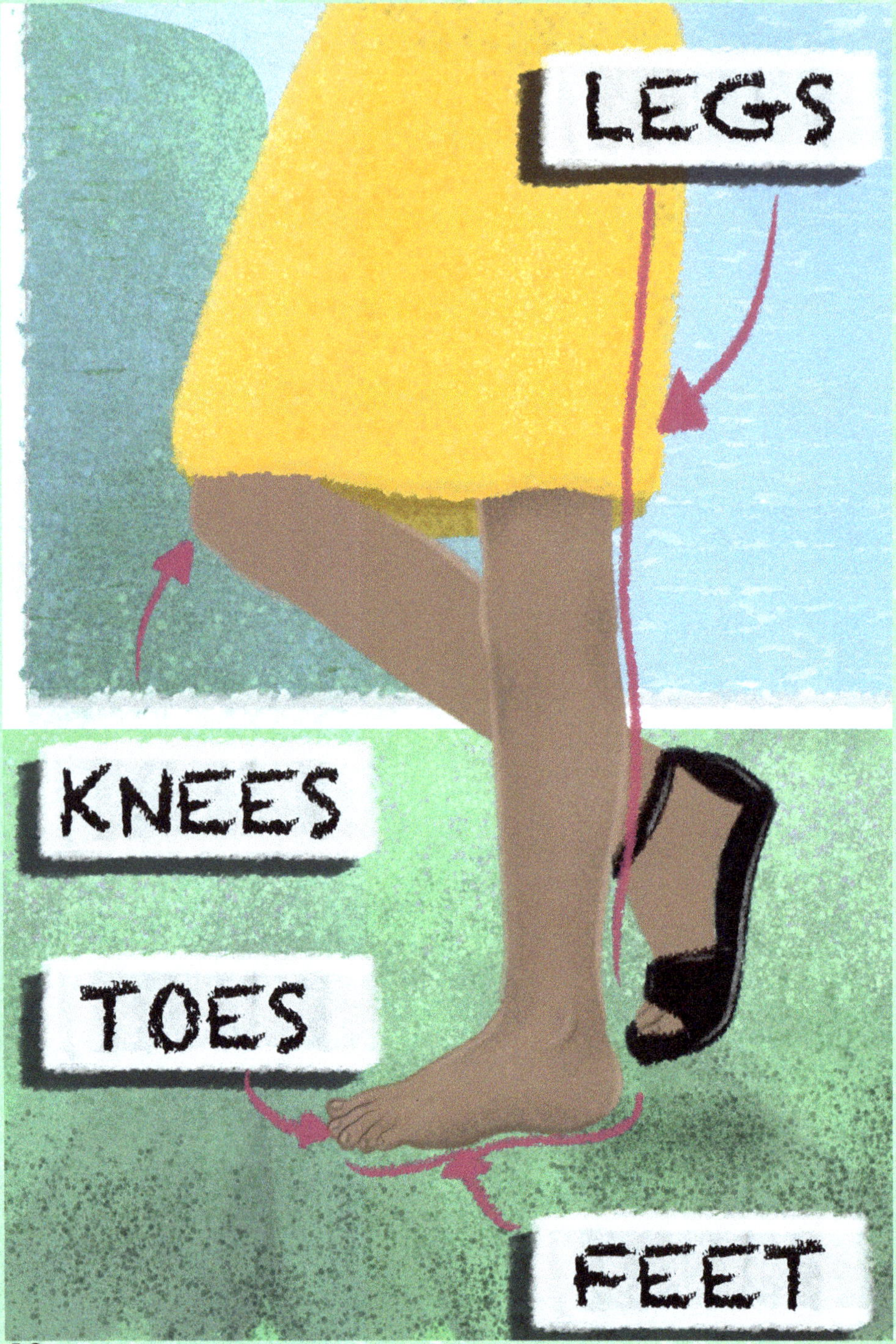
LEGS
KNEES
TOES
FEET

How about your
legs
knees
feet and
toes?

Now comes the tricky part.

Do you know the things that are inside your body?

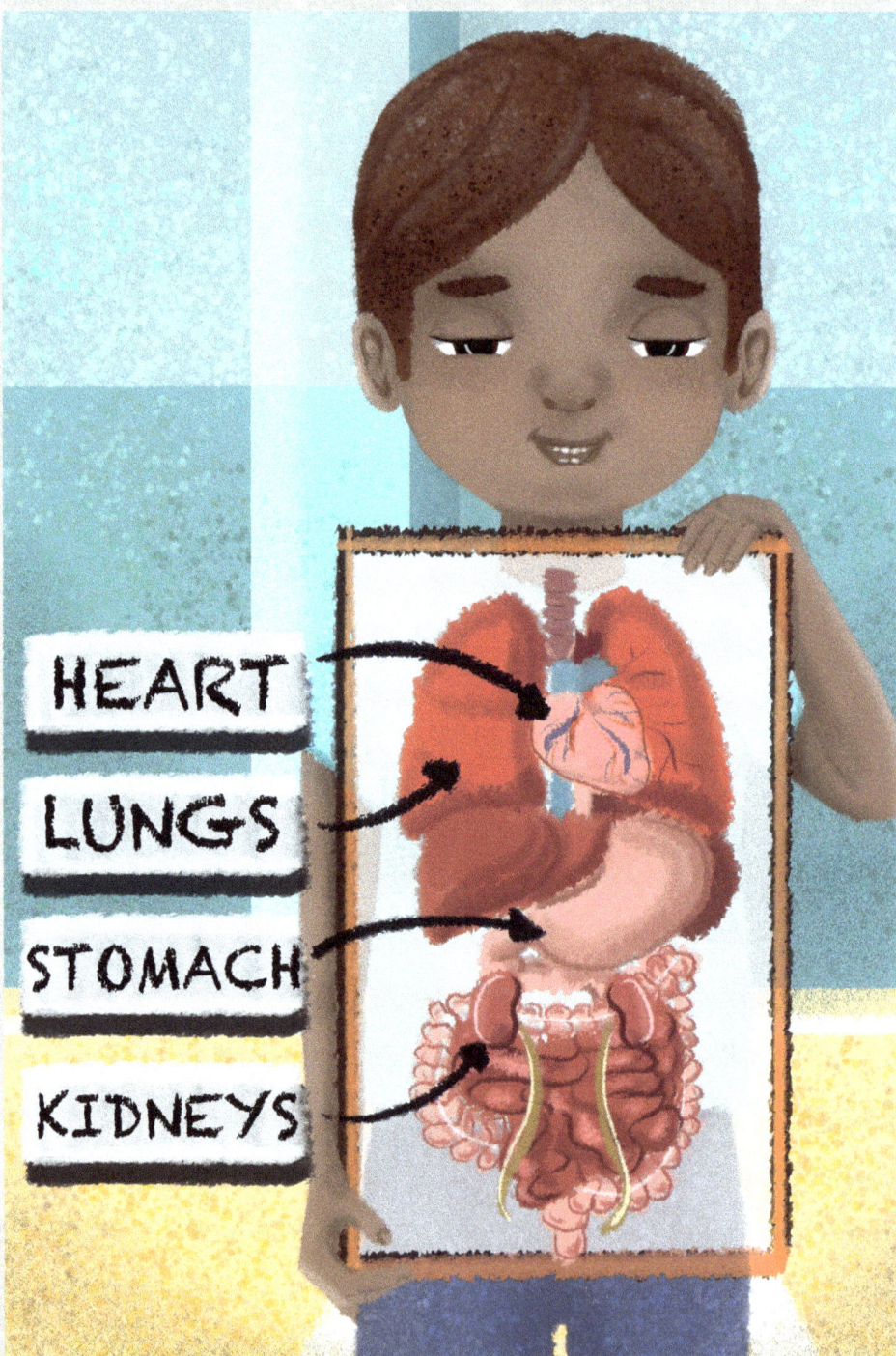

HEART

LUNGS

STOMACH

KIDNEYS

Under your skin you have a
heart
stomach
lungs and
kidneys.

And don't forget the bones!

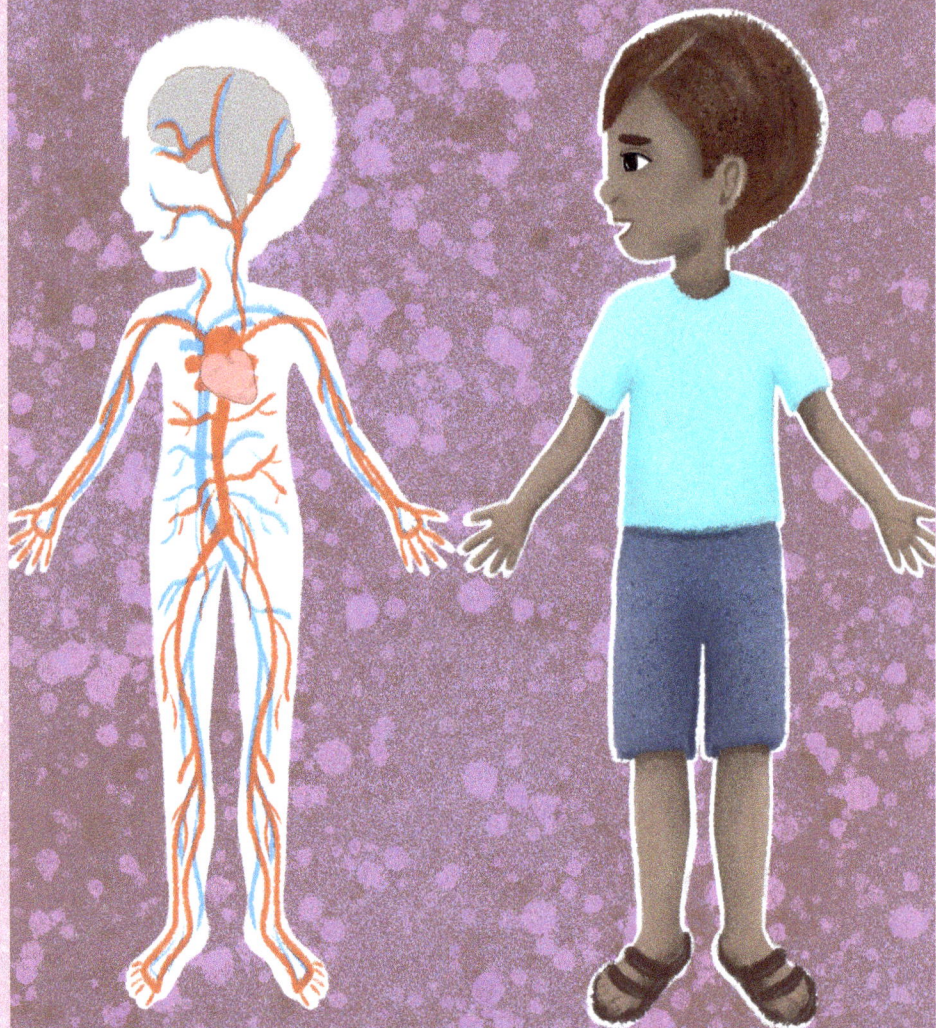

Blood vessels make sure every part of your body gets oxygen, and that vitamins go to all of your organs, your brain and your skin.

Your body is amazing!

You can use these questions to talk about this book with your family, friends and teachers.

What did you learn from this book?

Describe this book in one word. Funny? Scary? Colourful? Interesting?

How did this book make you feel when you finished reading it?

What was your favourite part of this book?

download our reader app
getlibraryforall.org

About the author

JOwen is from the Nurrunga/Ngarrindjeri Nations of South Australia. She was born in Adelaide and now lives in Broome, Western Australia. She loves the laughs and fun of family gatherings. As a child her favourite book was *I Can Jump Puddles.*

Our Yarning

Want to discover more books from this collection? Our Yarning is a collection of books written by Aboriginal and Torres Strait Islander peoples across Australia.

We know that children learn better, and enjoy reading more, when they see themselves in the stories, characters and illustrations of the books they read.

To download the app, visit the Google Play Store on any Android device and search 'Our Yarning'.

libraryforall.org